AF255277

Fear of 'Auditors'

Authority is Not Your Enemy.

How you can overcome fear of authority and be a winner.

Authority in:

- *Parenting.*
- *Schools.*
- *Colleges.*
- *Government.*
- *Organizations.*

Tawonga Muzah

Copyright © 2017. All rights reserved.

No part of this publication may be reproduced, stored in a retrieval system or transmitted in any way by any means, electronic, mechanical, photocopy, recording or otherwise, without the prior permission of the author except as provided by USA copyright law.

The opinions expressed by the author are not necessarily those of Revival Waves of Glory Books & Publishing.

Published by Revival Waves of Glory Books & Publishing

PO Box 596 | Litchfield, Illinois 62056 USA

www.revivalwavesofgloryministries.com

Revival Waves of Glory Books & Publishing is committed to excellence in the publishing industry.

Book design Copyright © 2017 by Revival Waves of Glory Books & Publishing. All rights reserved.

Published in the United States of America

Paperback: 978-1-365-99629-0

Table of contents

DEDICATION

To my lovely wife Nyasha Muzah and son Tawonga Jnr Muzah, and my mom Mrs. Maruva Rose Muzah and my brothers Takudzwa, Tapiwa and Baba Maita and family. Love you so much.

Introduction

A lot has been said about fear. Another writer described it as, "false evidence appearing real". Fear paralyses you and stops you from achieving your goals. It is a feeling that one has when in danger. Some fear when they suspect danger, some fear the unknown and some have this feeling from doubt or lack of faith. But living in fear is something that robs you of your happiness and success.

Many fears for people in authority come from the fear of being found wanting. It is a cause of concern that we attempt to clear this fear by alluding that to be corrected and disciplined is something that has an advantage to us as humans. Hebrews 12:11 say that no discipline seems pleasant at the time, but painful. Later on, however, it produces a harvest of righteousness and peace for those who are trained by it. So why fear to be corrected when it leads to our own peace.

A lot of times people who are in authority are judged wrongly. They are judged as people in search for those to punish and their love is not perceived. But if a Father tells a son not to touch fire, it is always out of love and the knowledge that he will be burnt. Hebrews 12:5-6 says "And you have forgotten that word of encouragement that addresses you as sons:" My son do not make light of the Lord's discipline and do not lose heart when he rebukes you, because the Lord disciplines those he loves and he punishes everyone he accepts as a son."

Fear of Auditors is therefore a motivational, inspiring book to pinpoint the dangers of rebelling against authority and an attempt to overcome fear by obedience or compliance and also to look at those in authority with the right eye.

Chapter 1:
ORIGINS OF AUTHORITY AND RULES AND THE PRESENT.

Devine Authority

Devine authority is based on love. It is a connection with the source of life, our creator. Everybody was born for a reason and God had a plan is his mind on your purpose and destiny. Whatever you bring into the world was shaped way before you were born. Jeremiah 1:5, "before I formed you in the belly, I knew you, and before you came out of the womb I sanctified thee, and I ordained thee a prophet unto the nations".

I was told a story about my birth one day by my mother .She said that, a "strange" person announced my birth to my grandmother who was in the rural areas. I was born April 30 1983, together with my twin brother Tarupiwa Muzah. My Mother and Father were surprised to see Granny arriving at the hospital and they questioned her saying how did she know about the birth. She said a "strange person" came and announced twins had been born to the family. Was this an angel, nobody knows. I guess this was God showing his power and stamping his authority on my life.

But that was not enough, another miracle happened, my twin brother who was last to come out, came out with bottom first and they were fears of the damage that the breech would do to my mother because of the existing lack of preparations. God took charge again and he was born safely.

Many people have a story were you were rescued from something that was going to harm you or of receiving certain signs that shows divine control of your life. All this is there for eliminating fear about the future. Indeed, your future is in God's hands.

Whenever we are faced with fears of based on penalties or discipline from various authority figures. Go back to the one who is above them all. God has the final say, he is the one who is in control more than parents, teachers, bosses and police, and they are all given authority over you by him.

We must separate ourselves from the fear of authorities given power by God and embrace Devine authority.

Origin from the word of God

If we go back to creation, taking it from the word of God, we know the origin of authority was when the first law was given to men in the Garden of Eden. God said "You are free to eat from any tree in the garden, but you must not eat from the tree of the knowledge of good and evil, for when you eat of it you will surely die." We see here that our loving Father gave this rule out of love and communicated the dangers of not following the regulation.

After man's fall God who had created men to be close to him and to fellowship with him made efforts to make that relationship possible. One of the efforts was giving the Ten Commandments to Moses and these rules were to be followed by his chosen people and it had promises of blessings but with curses if not followed accordingly. Rules and laws from Moses gave birth to Law and order being followed by the Judiciary systems of nations up to today.

These laws from God goes beyond physical laws, he also gives us trustworthy laws for our everyday life that provide strength, comfort and discernment for the immature. Precepts and norms are there that God gives to govern culture and society but it depends on how people apply these norms. There are no separate secular and sacred realms, all truth is God's truth and God gives us guidelines to the use of talents, gifts and resources that he gave us.

Psalms 19:14 must be our response to God, "may the words of my mouth and the meditation of my heart be pleasing in your sight, Lord my Rock and my Redeemer". Everything I think and say must honor God, the source of my emotions, motivation and action, must be also pleasing to God. So we must appreciate all laws, physical, social or moral as God's laws, and use them responsibly in his service.

Present state of authority

Today we have rules set by government, we have rules in the family, and we have rules everywhere. They are governing authorities that give us guidance in every aspect of our lives, be it business, at work, at church, in your family or in society. "Everyone must submit himself to the governing authorities, for there is no authority except that which God has established". (Romans 13:1)

Are men capable of following rules and regulations?

Can we say that it is in Adam's nature not to obey rules or can we say that Eve was to blame that she was weak to resist the devil that persuaded her to eat the fruit? Man was formed in God's image so it was in him to do well and to follow given rules and regulations but it is the influence of the devil that caused the fall of men in the Garden of Eden.

Why Authority, why rules?-Rules are out of love: Jesus' side

Jesus came as a source of salvation, God showed his love to us by justifying us through the death and resurrection of his son. Now the laws are put into our heart when we are born again. He is above every authority and his kingdom is everlasting. He defeated the penalty of our sin, defeated death on the cross, so that all who believe in him are given eternal life. Colossians 1;16 says For by him all things were created; things in heaven and on earth, visible and invisible, whether thrones or powers or rulers or authorities, all things were created by him and for him.

Jesus then commanded us to love one another saying he who loves has fulfilled the law, read Romans 13; 8. He says all laws given in Ten Commandments is summed up by one rule, "love your neighbor as yourself" (verse 9). So we see rules are love. We cannot live in peace without living in love. Jesus did not destroy the law; he summed it up in love. So we conclude that rules are given out of love.

Today accept Jesus Christ as your lord and savior, he will give you his love and put it in your heart, to enable you to follow rules and regulations out of love.

Problems from lack of Authority

Without parental authority we have problems like children getting pregnant whilst at school, some becoming criminals, some entering in fields like prostitution and others spending the rest of their lives in Jail. Children from single parents' families face trouble in lack of Father figures. It's all in the way a child was raised up that he or she becomes a product on environment and experiences.

Parental authority, the beginning of authority-helps you discover who you are

I was so good in math in pre -school; daddy always encouraged me to do it. I remember the games we used to play; most of them had an appreciation of some mathematics .Parental authority starts from the early stages of child development.

My Father was a teacher, so we benefited from a wide range of books. I liked this English book which had small words and big words. This developed a passion of writing for me.

My Father always brought books to read home. I then discovered a love for mathematics and maintained first position at Primary school. I had so much passion in mathematics beginning high school and started reading form two books whilst in form one. My father and mother always encouraged me and always made sure they provided everything needed for my growing passion.

Parents play an important role in the discovery of potential from the early stages of life. But children have to learn to obey their parents all the way in all stages of growing up. There is obviously a price of obedience that they have to pay through endurance and fighting peer pressure.

Chapter 2:
ENDURANCE –THE PRICE OF OBEDIENCE.

Sometimes you are faced with a fight whilst you are busy paying the price of obedience. I passed Mathematics exams of my end of form one examinations.

One early morning a colleague Pee came and asked me, 'Are you the one receiving the math price?'' I said yes, and then he continued, "How much did you score?" I had scored 97 percent as my final mark. PEE now a Medical doctor, went on and recalculated his math marks and found out that instead of a 95 percent that was on his record, the teacher did not given him an additional three marks for a certain question. He concluded saying, "I am the one getting the price" .Pee was the best student in the class but not in mathematics. Nobody could believe me to be the best in such a subject.

Fighting discouragement

This was to be the first discouragement and fight. I was in tears, went and told everyone in my class about what Pee was about to do. It was against rules that a final mark could be changed for another after it had been recorded. So other students went to my side and compelled the teacher to ignore Pee's request because he wanted to take advantage of me.

I fought so hard not to be discouraged by other people who were jealous of me, endured the pain. When you set out to be a good person who follows rules and submit to authority from parents, teachers, and society, you always make enemies, those who are jealous of you. You must focus and go on controlling your emotions even though you lose friends.

2 Timothy 2:3 says endure hardship as a good soldier of Christ Jesus. Verse 5 says, "If anyone competes as an athlete, he does not receive the victor's crown unless he competes according to rules".

Rules need endurance

Rules can be painful for us to comply in any setting but we see that victory for an athlete comes when he wins according to set rules. Many of us are looking forward to succeed. We love the happiness we have after succeeding. But we shun the pain of following the rules set in play. No pain no gain. God is teaching us that we have to get in a process of sacrifice and get in his strategy. God's ways are not our ways. God does things in a system. There are systems in business, systems in family, in society and in life. God created in everything a seed .A seed inside a tree. A seed is inside of you. THERE IS A FUTURE INSIDE OF YOU. There is a song ready to be written, a book to be finished. DONT LET ANYBODY TELL YOU, YOU ARE TOO OLD.

I AM HERE TO TELL YOU, YOU ARE PREGNANT, and when your season comes, you are going to make it. But there is pain in CHILD BIRTH. Pain when that seed dies .There is no way the seed is going to be a fruit until it dies. So the process of dying is the pain that needs endurance. It is when you act according to rules. When rules say fast and pray, to get a breakthrough. You ignore the pain and do what has been said.

Even when you face peer pressure to do other things that are against WHAT IS GOOD, what you are told to do by your advisors, your parents and those in Authority, You must endure, fight and have an attitude of a winner.

Peer PREASURE

Peer pressure is a way of mob psychology. Being gifted in a certain area you must follow the rules and be the best. Be an expert and your tomorrow will not have sorrow. Peers are a form of cultural authority that is normally ignored by parents who are so eager to see development in their child. Peers give you a way of life, lifestyle that has consequences tomorrow.

Music became another passion for me. I was a rising star and thought it was good to write music at the expense of reading and going to study in the library and writing assignments. This began a trouble in my life. I was nicknamed for never visiting the library. There was nothing wrong with music but everything wrong in not going for study in the library.

I passed my high school ,ordinary level and had an A in mathematics but was so famous at school in music but began dream of nothing else than my music. I lost focus in school and began focusing on nothing else but my music and growing fame. Only my parents were my hope. My peers were my confusion. I graduated from high school and enrolled at M.S.U College for a Degree in Physics but that was a wrong field for me.

I grew a wrong attitude towards school and towards my parents all because of peer pressure and lack of focus. This led to a rebellious spirit within me. I started to see my parents like they were fighting my real dream.

Perception is the fuel of every fear. It is how you look at something that determines the way you react to it. A lot has been said about perception, but to see things from the side of those guiding you is a complete turn from your wrong attitude. Be in their eyes, they see potential of even more than your present condition. Wrong attitude and feeling afraid that parents want to take other dreams away from you will make you disobey your parents.

Obedience and Disobedience

One day after passing my o levels, my parents were so happy that they asked me to come for a chat in the bedroom. They asked me, "What is the combination you will take in senior year." I said," What do you mean?" they continued, "We mean you are so good in mathematics, so we thought you must do Accounting as one of the subjects". I replied to my father and said, "Everything is okay". In my mind was my peers and my fame, little did my parents know about my rising music fame at school. I agreed to go register Accounting, Geography and Mathematics.

I went to school and found out that my peers had taken and registered science subjects instead. I disobeyed my parents and registered Physics Chemistry and Mathematics without alerting them. This became my downfall to be.

Sometimes disobedience seems not a sin, sometimes it feels okay. It's your life after all who has the right to govern it. But the bible says, "Honor your Father and Mother this has a promise that more years will be added to your life". Honor them, obey them, they see potential in you. I delayed my real assignment and destiny by killing an inside dream. I lacked the attitude of a winner and did not focus on my abilities.

Attitude of a winner

A winner is a person that follows through. Winners never quit and quitters never win. Here we are talking about attitudes. Different people have different attitudes towards authority and this defines whether they succeed in the different set ups and become happy.

You have to change your attitude towards those people who govern you. This is the purpose of this book. The process of changing attitude needs a communicator. Someone must communicate for you to have an understanding and change your perception towards some things. This process can be conceived as including for possible elements, a communicator, a communication, a subject and a group.

A communicator is a person who is attempting to persuade someone.

A communication, the information or the message intended to persuade.

A subject is the target of the persuasion attempt.

A group is that of which the subject is a member.

So I am the communicator and you reading this book, my subject.

Two twins were brought up by an alcoholic and one became an alcoholic and the other not. The alcoholic was asked, "you were brought up by an alcoholic, why are you alcoholic, he replied, 'because I was brought up by an alcoholic". The other twin was asked why he was not an alcoholic and he gave the same answer, "Because I was brought up by an alcoholic".

Attitude is the drive that can make you a winner. You have to harness the power to win by having the right attitude all the way.

The Bible also talks about this in Jude saying people who talk negatively about things they don't understand. When your attitude is to despise authority, you talk bad about it. You talk negative about all the principles that are there to govern you and make you reach places of fulfillment.

Come on be a winner, follow through, inspired by all in front of you, including all the regulations which are to be adhered to.

Me I also used to be this bad boy, with a bad boy attitude towards education in my life. If I was told go to class and not to run away from lessons, I would say no then do what I want. But the more I broke simple rules, the more I failed until I dropped out. I latter changed my attitude towards school, enrolled at another college and that was beginning of something else.

Master your attitude. There is that emotion that comes from lack of knowledge which is there just to destroy you. My people are destroyed for lack of knowledge. BE it attitude towards your job, your wife, your church or your business. Change it by acquiring the right information as to how to succeed and follow it through.

Just because you are in a certain place don't mean you have the right attitude. YOU can be like JUDAS, he was with Jesus but that did not mean he was a good person, he ended up betraying Jesus in the end. Check your heart, do you have the right attitude, or you have hate or bitterness hidden in you.

All these sins of the heart destroy your initiatives. You have all the talent in the world; you have all the dreams, visions, all the anointing but you are spoiled by your attitude.

How can you be happy under authority? - Work on relationships with people.

Horizontal relationship is whereby you work out your love for your fellow brothers and sisters. Don't work out your relationship with God only. In the Bible God said, how can you love God that you don't see and hate your brother you see? Many live in hate; thereby shun authority all because of hate. You don't listen to a person you hate whether they are in authority or not. Hate has caused wars, people against authority in their nations. Avoid conflict. Be a person willing to obey and listen to others so that you live in peace. The bible also tells us to follow peace with all men.

Children, you must have good relationships with your parents. The rules and discipline is not a thing to make you hate them. If they don't correct you, the police will, the court rooms will, the jail will. It's better to listen than to meet challenges later in life. Management and subordinates, is there a relationship between boss and employee? LETS ALL BE IN PEACE AND BE FREE by finding ways to conquer and fight our fears.

Chapter 3:
WAYS TO CONQUER FEAR–FEAR OF AUTHORITY

Use the word of God

Contrary to what some may believe, worry is not a harmless emotion you can afford to entertain in your life. Worry is a form of fear that will subtly find its way into your mind, will, and emotions, causing you to make decisions that are not faith-based. When your mind is constantly bombarded with concerns, cares and fear-based thoughts, your faith is paralyzed and you put yourself in a position to see the things you don't want to happen to come to pass. I believe it is time for a complete overhaul in this area of our thinking, particularly in the times in which we live.

This book will help you make this shift. Just like faith comes by hearing the Word of God, worry comes by hearing and receiving words that contradict the Word. It is not God's will for you to worry about anything. Constantly people are worried about rules and regulations, whether they are fit to comply or obey and the penalties that arise from not obeying. They see their lives as a fight with curses and spirits that are punishments of their misbehaviors.

2 Timothy 1:7 lets us know fear is a spirit that does not come from God. Therefore, any form of fear, including worry, is natural and should not be tolerated on any level. Allowing fearful and anxious thoughts to take up residence in your mind opens the door for that spirit to invade every area of your life. Often what starts out as a small concern can balloon into a full –blown fear that you never had before. Keep in mind fear has a sibling called torment. This is why fear is connected with a nagging sense of unrest. This is a clear sign of the enemy's torment.

Use these verses from the Bible and meditate and speak them at the beginning of everyday after your morning prayers.

Psalms 27:1-The Lord is my light and my salvation, whom shall I fear? The lord is the strength of my life, of whom shall I be afraid?

Psalms 56:3-What time I am afraid, I will trust in thee.

Psalms 56:11-In God have I put my trust: I will not be afraid what man can do to me.

Mathew 14:25-27-And in the fourth watch of the night Jesus went unto them, walking on the sea. And the disciples saw him walking on the sea, they cried out for fear. But straightaway Jesus spoke unto them saying. Be of good cheer, it is I; Be not afraid.

Romans 8:31-What shall we then say to these things. If God is for us, who can be against us?

2 Timothy 1:7-For God hath not given us the spirit of fear, but of power and of love, and of a sound mind.

1 John 4:8-There is no fear in love, but perfect love cast out fear: because fear hath torment. He that fears is not made perfect in love.

Replace fear with Courage

From the Bible, Romans 12:4 says," Authority is a terror to those who do wrong". So if you want to overcome this fear, it can only be by obedience and doing what is right.

We always had a fear back in High school for this English literature Teacher named Mr. Ganzo. He required us to memorize a line from the novel Julius Caesar and share it every time before the lesson starts, he often said, "if you don't come up with something, you are going to get three strokes". Many students got these strokes of his leather belt in every of his lesson periods and that made Mr. Ganzo to be feared.

But one day I had courage to overcome my fears. It seemed he was in search for more students to give his strokes all the time. So I wanted to really find out. I began memorizing many lines from the book. As time went on I found out that all the fear I once had for Mr. Ganzo was replaced by so much love for him. I was so eager to meet him every time he had a lesson period with our class. I would present my lines to an applauding class and became the best student and latter passed the subject with flying colors.

So you see by this story that people in authority are judged wrongly. Mr. Ganzo just wanted us to develop our knowledge of the book by making us memorize lines from the book. He knew that would make us pass. We mistaken him for a very hard and cruel teacher and feared him so much. But when I replaced fear with courage, I leant to look at what is being instructed. You have to focus on the advantages of doing what you are being told to do. Is it adding anything to your happiness? So yes go for it. It's not about who is instructing you and giving you the rules; it's about what you benefit from complying with what is laid for you to follow.

Respect and Fear

Respect is actually acknowledging someone for his talents and abilities; not fearing someone. We respect our parents because they are able to take care for us. We honor God for who he is. We respect management and our leaders in various aspects of our lives. We don't have to see their bad side or cruelty or toughness. We see their good character and their love. I ended up respecting my Literature teacher and saw that he loved me. His discipline was a form of strategy to make me do as he wanted me to, so as to reap the benefits in future.

Communication is the key

Communication is the conveying of information from the sender to the receiver who must give a perceived feedback.

In organizations information can be exchanged regarding the operations of an enterprise through communication ideas, facts and emotions can be interchanged between two or more people using words, letters and symbols.

Clarity, attention, integrity and choice of media must all be considered for effective communication

Processes of ,framing a message for transmission, transmitting the message, receiving the message, ensuring that the message has reached its destination and then ensuring that some desired action has been produced as a result of receiving the message which has been communicated must all be taken into consideration.

In the field of Auditing, communication is greatly a necessity, something every Auditor must be so much good at. Authority requires good communication. For those under leadership to meet deadlines, to meet targets and to have outputs according to objectives set by visionaries, it must all be communicated through manuals and guidelines. Auditors come in to assess that those guidelines are being followed religiously. The problem is that some people are ignorant of what must be done. It has not been communicated to them. As a result, this lack of communication will trigger fear of authorities when they are required to appraise management or authorities on current states or situations of inefficiency. Let's not just punish people who lack knowledge of regulations.

1 Timothy 5:7, Give the people these instructions too, so that no one may be open to blame.

In government statutory instruments are put in gazette for public to read and understand the rules and regulations so they comply in different ministries.

What are you doing in your organization to make sure they have knowledge to the dot on all controls set and all rules and regulations? We don't want to paralyze people in fear because of ignorance of laws because of lack of communication.

Chapter 4:
AUTHORITY FIGURES, 'AUDITORS'

Organizational Authority

Nations are governed by constitutions, statutory instruments are drawn also from the constitutions and handbooks of regulations for various ministries also are drawn to make up the regulations to be followed. Companies are also governed by constitutions as well as manuals of rules and regulations that must be followed by different departments.

Internal Auditors

Internal auditing is an appraising tool to appraise management on effectiveness and efficiency of internal controls advising on risk management processes. Internal controls are controls set by management to achieve objectives in an organization.

External auditors look at financial statements as a whole and give assurance to public, investors and shareholders whether they show a true or fair view.

It is therefore not a duty of Auditors to detect fraud. So the belief that auditors run around looking for fraud is a traditional view of auditing. Auditors come to see if the rules are being adhered to and to communicate to management the deficiencies and give recommendations as to on measures to be taken to make controls effective.

So you see there is no reason to fear Auditors when their primary concern is not even to detect fraud, all that traditional view of Auditors create the fear that people normally have. Auditors are part of management; they are the ears of management.

At this other institution that was audited by some of my fellows at work. After the first day when they met the management for a pre audit meeting, they woke up tomorrow and the office of the accountant was in flames and all the records were burnt. This was an obvious method to destroy records and hide evidence that could lead to prosecution because of Fraud. So if you have done something wrong, you fear but when all is good, there is no reason to fear authorities.

Authority in family set up.

Parents

Another writer shared a story about his mother who used to beat him so hard after stealing some things in the house. He said after growing up for some time ,he had a chance to visit one jail cell and found out the conditions in these cells and the kind of life people locked there were experiencing. That made him think all that chastening that he thought was cruel to him was helpful and because it was meant to prevent him for the punishment by other authorities in the future.

I had an experience once with my Father; he had things he wanted to tell us that were wrong. I silently set in the sofa waiting for him to finish. He expected us to freeze and show the fear cause of the corrections .I stood up and went to my bedroom and came back with this magazine which had the same things he was rebuking us with. And I said, "Dad you are a genius, wow! You went word to word, did you read this?" My attitude towards discipline or correction was that of development and not of it as a cruel means of showing who is ruling who.

Sounds familiar right, yes, this is the attitude in most homes, whether its husband and wife, of Father and son, it's a battle of supremacy rather that an opportunity of advancement and knowledge and development.

Many of the times parents raise emotions in children and children develop wrong perceptions.

The way they see you must change. IT MUST be communicated to them that you love them so much and whatever commandment you are giving to them has so much help in the future.

I used to hate it when my mother forced me to go till the garden. I am now using those skills at my house and my beautiful wife Nyasha loves it too, and am looking forward for my son Tawonga Junior to learn about it too. Many divorces are as a result of rebellion that happened when children ignored principles that parents tried to instill, principles of love, peace, work, trust ,honesty and security all that are taught at tender ages.

Our senses are deceived by what our minds are directed to see, feel or hear, in an extreme state of suggestibility. So we must change our thoughts. Change your thinking.

Parental acceptance more in discipline helps

Even in development and learning, Parental acceptance will have an obvious effect upon the child's emotional readiness to learn. Being confident of his ability's worth and feeling secure in his parents' affection even if he fails to attain perfection, the child will be willing to undertake the learning of morality and other tasks. So parents help to change thoughts of children by accepting them and praising them so they know and understand your love and care and develop self-confidence. Without feeling of security, the most powerful man in the world will be anxious and fearful.

Many parents however have a belief that a well-brought –up child is one whose spirit has been broken, who is timid rather than brave, helpless rather than self-confident. In the interests of discipline, they ignore the natural rhythm of the child's dependence drives, satisfying them according to some arbitrary schedule. You have to praise your child, give him names of victory and be friendly to them to avoid having obedient children with inner misery.

Ephesians 6:1, says, Children, obey your parents in the lord, for this is right. Verse 4, Fathers do not exasperate your children, instead bring them up in the training and institution of the Lord.

Husband and wife

In marriages it is a traditional method that a Father has to be feared. Husbands come back after work and expects his food on the table and he does not talk to anyone and also beats the wife if there is no food prepared. Recent, modern marriages applaud communication and respect is natural and not exaggerated. Family finances are managed by both wife and husband and there is no fear but respect and family live Kingdom life.

Husbands need respect, Wives need love.

Ephesians 5:33, however each one of you also must love his wife as he loves himself and the wife must respect his husband.

Just respecting your husband by saying, "How was work daddy?" washing his hands; cooking dinner and ironing his clothes go a long way. Complementing your wife saying," you are beautiful", and loving her, listening to her and buying gifts also does the same for your wife.

Husbands love your wife as Christ loved the church and gave himself up for her. The two shall become one flesh, a profound mystery talking about Christ and the church. This taken from Ephesians in the bible shows us how much love we talking about. Now why do husbands find it difficult to listen to their wives and do what they are asked to do, when Jesus Christ is alive now making sure all our requests in prayer are answered? He gave up everything about him to do for his bride, the church. Stop being busy watching soccer and attend to your beautiful wife.

To sum it all up, Ephesians 5:22-25, Wives, submit to your husband's as to the lord, For the husband is the head of the wife as Christ is the head of the church, his body, of which he is the Savior. Now as the church submits to Christ, so also wives should submit to their husbands in everything.

Policemen

We need police officers to control crime. A person is, bylaw, innocent until proven guilty at trial in a court. An arrest is made when a person is suspected of having committed a crime. If a police officer thinks a person has committed a crime, he will go to a magistrate or Justice of the Peace to get permission to arrest him. This permission is a written order called a warrant. A police officer either gets evidence that a person has committed a crime, goes to Judge or magistrate of the Peace to ask for a warrant, states what crime he thinks the person has committed. A warrant is an order instructing all police officers to arrest the person named and bring him before the court to be charged with that specific offence.

A police officer will find the person and give him the warrant.

Officers do not arrest a person if there is no reason to suspect that they have committed a crime. So there is no fear that you can be arrested when you did not do any crime.

Police can arrest without a warrant if he sees you committing an offence or there is good evidence to show that a certain person is a criminal and believes going to get a warrant can cause the person to escape, hide some evidence, or interfere with witnesses. By declaration of rights you have protection from human treatment, so beatings not much allowed but a form of force is allowed when necessary. Avoid to be caught in the wrong side of the law, but don't fear anyone just because he is in a uniform.

Teacher discipline

Discipline refers to a set of rules or norms, specifying acceptable forms of conduct, which is either imposed by authorities and people or agreed between them. It is a form of social control.

For Teachers, skills in empathy are an obvious help in understanding the pupils' attitudes and motives, placing the teacher in a markedly advantageous position for selecting an appropriate control technique that will help the child to grow, rather than merely putting a stop to the misbehavior, which is the teacher's most pressing need. This approach makes Teachers to be liked rather than feared.

Religious Authority

God gave the Jews the Ten Commandments and many other laws at Mount Sinai. These laws taught the people how to worship God and live holy lives. Jesus later told the Jews that following rules was important, but loving God and others was important. Him being the head of the body, he has set apostles, prophets, teachers, pastors and evangelists all in Authority together with him in the church which is his body. In church there is also leadership from Bishops, Overseers, District pastors, to elders and deacons. Books of rules and regulations are also written to govern churches and many disciplinary issues are discussed and dealt with in district and provincial councils.

Chapter 5:
HOW DO YOU CONTROL YOUR EMOTIONS WHEN DEALING WITH AUTHORITY?

Be willing to handle reproof

Your administrator is not always right, but he generally has a pretty good handle on things. Be willing to listen to him. Accept what he says. Don't be guilty of listening without hearing. Admit it if you are wrong. Attempt to change or correct the situation.

You will find that most suggestion or corrections are not personal confrontations. They are an effort to strengthen the total program. The end result is a better equipped person.

The best reproof is to admit your own problems. Request help in solving them. When the help is given, follow it.

Face the emotion

Emotions need not to be eliminated, they can be controlled. Fear is a pure state of non-adjustment, and has no utility that can be discovered. The person who boasts of being fearless and danger doubles his burden of fear. He not only fears the real danger but also fears being found out. Such additional sources of emotion can be avoided by facing the fact that you are afraid.

Reinterpret Situation

The third thing to do is reinterpret the situation. An emotion is a product of interpretation. It is not a stimulus-in-itself, but a stimulus-as-interpreted, that triggers an emotional reaction.

For example, a child will show fear if dropped, but if its father does the dropping with a clucking laugh it will respond with delight. An adult employee therefore, who is frightened by a request to appear to Head office can reduce his emotion by realizing that the request may be motivated not by displeasure but by a need for information. Reinterpretations are not easy to make. Sometimes a person may need the help of an objective; imaginative thinking. Sometimes a person may need an objective outsider in order to see his own difficult situation from a different point of view.

Sometimes a situation is too urgent to permit long-term reinterpretation. In such cases, the ability to see the situation with humor or detached realism can be of help. Laughter even when unjustified helps to relieve emotional tension.

Realism keeps people from taking themselves too seriously. Part of the releasing effect of humor is due to the fact that any activity helps to relieve the tension of emotion .The extra energy provided by the inner changes of emotion must be used up. That's, a good rule for immediate relief is to engage in activity. The old ideas of running round the block or chopping wood to 'work off steam' are psychologically sound.

Perform an activity correcting situation

The best way to resolve an emotional condition is to perform an activity that is directly useful in correcting the provoking situation. It is easier to attack a problem than to control one's feeling about it. For example, instead of trying to control a general fear of losing a position, one should try to become expert in the job that concern over job security will be groundless.

Practice dealing with Problems

Feelings depend upon one's early estimate of one's relationship to any test situation. The well-prepared student welcomes an examination as an opportunity to prove himself; the unprepared student dreads a test. People who fear social situations can go a long way towards becoming confident by learning to master social amenities and skills. One's feelings depend very greatly upon such skills, and these can be developed and enlarged in scope by conscious thought and practice. Some problems are caused by those in authority who are not flexible in the rules they give to people. But you also must find a way of dealing with them.

Flexibility in setting rules

People should be considerate sometimes in setting rules, when auditing there was this other school that was from remote areas and their banks were very far. According to regulations, they are supposed to bank collected monies within fought eight hours. One day we went to Audit the institution and found out that they had not banked collected monies for months. I asked the accountant why, and he explained that it was because of the long distances from the banks. You see, so the rules available were not flexible to accommodate remote areas.

Sometimes we know they are rules that are given in a family set up, but there is need of flexibility when considering gifted children, who sometimes need to work long hours perfecting their gifts and talents. So sometimes these gifted children need encouragement from both parents and school authorities. Bible says cast your nets wide, you don't know whether you will make it on this or that. That's the reason why extracurricular activities are taught at school.

Entrepreneurship which has been long forgotten to be included in our early school curricular is also another area that deals with developing talents and abilities, but it must not conflict with schooling. But modern education must find a way to balance schooling, entrepreneurship and extracurricular activities like arts and culture.

At one time my father had to come to another college to stop me from performing in a music concert. I began fearing him, seeing him as an enemy to my gift in music. But it was a wrong perception because the school side for me was not yet well developed. I needed help, and found it from my parents.

You must find a way of balancing your motives, clearing every guilty feelings and trying to see to harness the attitude of a winner. Everything you have is a gift from God. James 1:17, every good gift and every perfect gift is from above, and cometh down from the father of lights, with whom no variableness, neither shadow of turning. It's from God, just find ways to balance everything that he has given you without strife. And don't be rebellious to those that are there to guide you. Don't fear authority, it is there to assess whether all controls are effective for you and you alone.

Chapter 6:
REBELLIOUS SPIRIT

I was rebellious to college rules. I was at Seventh Day Adventist University and one of the rules was gate passes. One day. The dean was not there to sign my pass one day. I forged his signature and went out of college and came back. This was discovered. I was going to be suspended.

I felt so ashamed of myself and so afraid of facing my parents who believed in me and my schooling. God did it again. We saw a sign at the basketball court seconds before a college worker came to tell us that we were wanted by the dean. Two girls were with me and my twin shooting hoops. We raised our voices and started shouting, "It's in, and it's in!" The ball was about to get down for a miss, then a miracle happened; it forcefully moved itself from going down and went into the ring.

These girls were so afraid of the sign that they started asking us were we going for church. There and there the college worker came and I knew because of the sign that we were not going to be suspended. The dean walked with us going to his office and went past another lecturer who asked jokingly, "Do you know the people you are walking with?" He said, "No I don't". The dean then latter said to us, "You are not going to be suspended but you now on punishment".

When you rebel against authority, you can never run away from punishment. We learned the hard way but God; the one who has all the authority controlled the situation, like he always does.

Hebrews 12:15-16, See to it that no one is sexually immoral, or is Godless like Esau, who for a single meal sold his inheritance rights as oldest son.

Rebellion is sin as witchcraft. Rebellion is to disobey and turn against those in authority. You see in Hebrews that Esau was supposed to be in the list of inheritors of God's blessing to his people Israel. He rebelled and turned against all these promises through his hunger.

Rebellion is often caused by a life lived without delayed gratification.

Hunger will pass, loneliness will pass, and the enemy tricks you into wanting to satisfy your fleshly desires at the expense of your destiny.

Jonah 1, 1-4

''Now the word of the lord came unto Jonah the son of Amittai, saying, arise, go to Ninevah, that great city, and cry against it; for their wickedness is come up before me. But Jonah rose up to flee unto Tarshish from the presence of the lord, and went down to Joppa; and he found a ship going to Tarshish: so he paid the fare thereof, and went down into it, to go with them unto Tarshish from the presence of the lord. But the Lord sent out a great wind into the sea, and there was a mighty tempest in the sea, so that the ship was like to be broken".

Jonah rebelled against the lord's commands and it did not go well with Him. God is in the business of sending his people to guide you through orders, rules and regulations. Don't be like Jonah, who was transported in the fish's belly to go and do the work.

How many people are like Esau and Jonah, who failed to obey certain orders, rules and regulations by wanting to enjoy the moment? The energy levels of excitement can rise if enticed. This rise in levels can only be controlled by calming yourself first, then getting more sides to the story. Many people are into calm and make decisions too fast and out of too much excitement. You need to carefully consider the advantages and disadvantages of your actions.

Some become liars and cheaters and robbers and enter into covenants with the devil because of their flesh. James 1:14, But every man is tempted, when he is drawn away by his own lust, and enticed. The devil enticed Eve to eat the fruit and disobey God. He is the one that makes you focus on pleasing your flesh at the expense of holiness and obedience.

Stupidity is giving away your future because of temporary things.

The devil is the owner of rebellion. Resist the devil and he will flee away from you. Change your attitude and don't protest against regulations in your society in family at your work place in your life.

Chapter 7:
REPENTANCE

I began drinking alcohol and smocking because of peer pressure at a very tender age. One day I was fed up of all of that. I was so drunk one Saturday and started speaking vulgar, insulting this sister who was walking past me going back home.

I woke up ashamed of myself. I guess it was the Holy Spirit rebuking me. It was on a Sunday, 22 June 2003. In my church, Zaoga Fif International, it is advised to know the date you were saved; you must remember if you are sure you were born again. I went to church smelling alcohol from yesterday's drinking.

The pastor preached from Colossians 3:8 about Christians who use vulgar and do bad things. It says, "But now you put off all these, anger, wrath, malice, blasphemy, filthy communication out of your mouth". Wow, the message was for me that day. Pastor went on saying, "Some of you are Christians but you go telling vulgar to other brothers and sisters, you get drunk and on Sunday come to church".

I saw myself walking to the pulpit and repented that day. God touched my heart. I had a complete change of mind. I went back home and told my brother, who was the only one at church from our family, not to tell anyone of my repentance. But my mother saw the change in me without hearing the story and gave me books to read for my developing love of God. From the books one favorite was called Good Morning Holy Spirit.

I went on reading books the whole day and praying in the evening. I went to a passage of scripture from Luke 11, which says, "If you then, being evil, know how to give good gifts to your children: how much more shall your heavenly Father give the Holy Spirit to them that ask". I began to ask God to give me the Holy Spirit, saying, "By the blood of Jesus, in the name of Jesus, God give me the Holy Spirit". I fell into something like a trance, opened my mouth and began speaking in tongues. I went to my knees to thank God of receiving the Holy Spirit that day. I remember saying good morning Holy Spirit early in the morning.

A lot of changes happened in my life including hearing God saying to me, "John six verse six" three times when sleeping one day. I was fasting and praying for 3 weeks. His voice in my sleep strengthened me and gave me confidence up to this day. Prophesies and visions followed, but it's not a surprise if you belong to a Pentecostal church.

A change of mind is a change of everything in your life. Invite God today, say," Jesus come into my heart. I believe you came and died on the cross for me and resurrected on the third day". God will change your life. His AUTHORITY IS IN HIS WORD, REPENT and follow the way, the truth and the life. Obey his commands now and live a blessed life. Be a WINNER.

If you read the story of the prodigal son in the bible you hear that he went back home again. This is repentance. Go back to your destiny. Go to obedience, to holiness and to submission to God and to love of every guidance and light in your life.

Sometimes Jesus in his ministry on earth always asked sick people, saying, do you want to be whole? Repent, and forgive yourself. Hebrews 12; 13, make level paths for your feet, so that the lame may not be disabled, but rather healed. Hebrews 12; 17, Afterward, as you know, when he wanted to inherit the blessing, he was rejected. He could bring about no change of mind, though he sought it with tears.

So sometimes people show emotion but that does not mean a change in mind. When you show emotion that you are doing badly, that's not a change of mind. Repentance means a change of mind, not your tears.

Esau sought to inherit the blessing by tears but his heart and mind did not change.

This book is meant to change your mind. Change your attitude towards the good and towards the right living that God wants for you. Don't hide bitterness, resentment and hate.

Be willing to submit to God, be willing to submit to authority. God can heal you; let it go, yield to someone's command, to God, your parents, and your company authorities. Humble yourself before God and he will lift you up.

Repentance is a change of mind; a shift in focus .I never had anything to do with Physics. I failed over and over again. It was time for change. Like the prodigal son he said enough is enough. I decided not to write my physics examination and drop out of the college. Part of this change of mind was led by God; he was in control and at that time. I went to another college and passed Accounting degree, recorded my music album that same time.

Repent and obey. What is it in your history that you think you were disobedient and rebellious. You still have a chance to repent. The prodigal son went back home. For me Accounting was home.

Change of attitude

I remember one day my father telling me to fight, I fought to change from Physics degree to Accounting degree. That was not enough. I had to learn to pass my modules. Then one day got hold of a book that talked about attitude. Attitude towards your teacher determines your passing at school. I said this is it. I started loving my lectures. The result was I feared no more. I was prepared for every lecture all the time, read in advance and listened and obeyed everything they said. This shift and repentance, change of mind, made me pass Accounting degree with good grades.

Change and Love

For the conclusion, 1 John 4:18," There is no fear in love; but perfect love cast out all fear: because fear hath torment. He that fears is not made perfect in love".

Among all my theory of fear of auditors, the opposite being love of auditors. My love for my lectures at college went a long way. My best lecturer was the one who taught us Auditing.

I went into this other class and set and heard him saying, "They are some students who are not supposed to be in this class but they are here, they have not yet passed the pre requisite of this module". He was talking about me. I had not yet passed

Accounting 2.2. I went out at that very moment and saw him smiling at my obedience.

I read and passed the Accounting module with high grades .If you repent and change your attitude, you will love authority. I work up one morning so excited to go meet my best lecturer. I woke up reading the book of Daniel in the bible. To my surprise when I got into class, my lecturer came in smiling and his first words were, "Class, lets open the book of Daniel ".This shows that it was God who directed me to be obedient and to succeed. I loved the module and passed with distinction BECAUSE OF MY LOVE FOR MY LECTURER AND WORKING HARD.

In everything prayer is the best remedy. God gives you peace that surpasses all understanding. Pray and let God show you your weaknesses, show you the way and make you be able to conquer every fear that fights your destiny, fears of authority from rebellion and disobedience that causes you not to make it in your life.

www.ingramcontent.com/pod-product-compliance
Lightning Source LLC
Chambersburg PA
CBHW071519030726
47593CB00003B/1330